NATIONAL GEOGRAPHIC | **GLOBAL ISSUES**

FOOD SUPPLY

Andrew J. Milson, Ph.D.
Content Consultant
University of Texas at Arlington

Acknowledgments

Grateful acknowledgment is given to the authors, artists, photographers, museums, publishers, and agents for permission to reprint copyrighted material. Every effort has been made to secure the appropriate permission. If any omissions have been made or if corrections are required, please contact the Publisher.

Instructional Consultant: Christopher Johnson, Evanston, Illinois

Teacher Reviewers: Leah Perry, Exploris Middle School, Raleigh, North Carolina
Erin Stevens, Quabbin Regional Middle/High School, Barre, Massachusetts

Photographic Credits

Cover, Inside Front Cover, Title Page ©Keren Su/Corbis. **3** (bg) ©David Toase/Stockbyte/Getty Images. **4** (bg) ©Steve Winter/National Geographic Stock. **6** (bg) ©REUTERS/Finbarr O'Reilly. **7** (tl) ©Jake Lyell/Alamy. **8** (bg) Mapping Specialists. **10** (bg) ©Hugh Sitton/Corbis. **11** (tl) ©REUTERS/Munish Sharma. **12** (cr) ©Amit Dave/Reuters/Corbis. **13** (bg) ©REUTERS/Stringer. **15** (bg) ©Janet Jarman/Corbis. **16** (bg) ©Atlantide Phototravel/Corbis. **19** (bg) ©Jean-Luc Manaud/Gamma-Rapho/Getty Images. **20** (bg) ©James Morris. (tr) ©Gavin Kingcome Photography/Garden Picture Library/Getty Images. **22** (bg) ©Marshall Burke. **23** (tl) ©Zacharie Sero Tamou. **24** (cr) ©Lennart Woltering. **25** (bg) ©Joerg Boethling/Alamy. **27** (t) ©Gage/Getty Images. **28** (tl) ©Gary K Smith/Garden Picture Library/Getty Images. **30** (tr) ©Janet Jarman/Corbis. (br) ©Jake Lyell/Alamy. **31** (bg) ©David Toase/Stockbyte/Getty Images. (tr) ©Joerg Boethling/Alamy. (br) ©REUTERS/Stringer. (bl) ©Edwin Remsberg/Getty Images.

For permission to use material from this text or product, submit all requests online at www.cengage.com/permissions.

Further permissions questions can be emailed to permissionrequest@cengage.com.

Visit National Geographic Learning online at www.NGSP.com.

Visit our corporate website at www.cengage.com.

Printed in the USA.

RR Donnelley, Jefferson City, MO

ISBN: 978-07362-97561

12 13 14 15 16 17 18 19 20 21

10 9 8 7 6 5 4 3 2 1

A Hungry WORLD

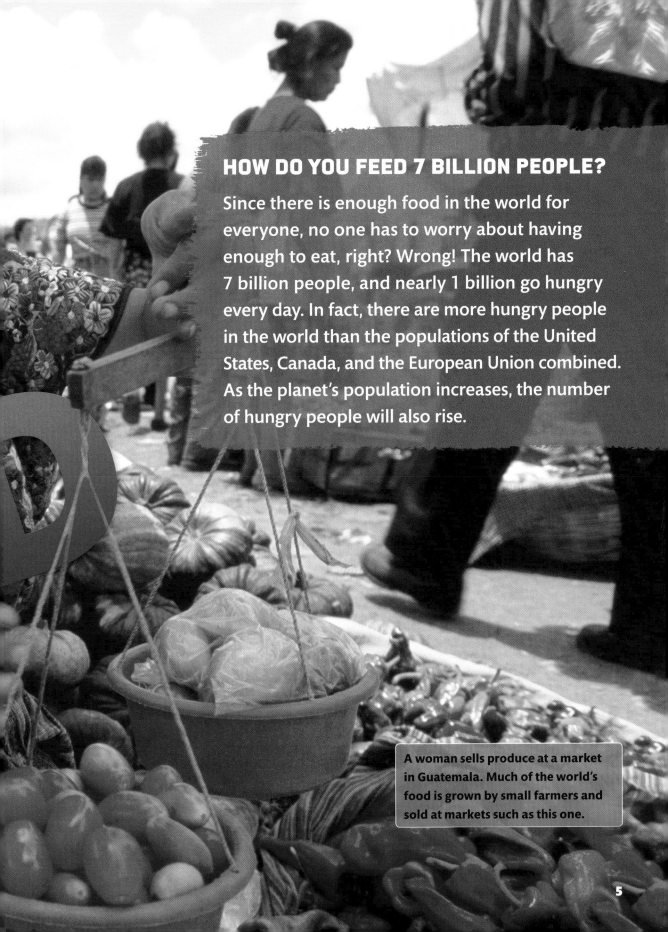

HOW DO YOU FEED 7 BILLION PEOPLE?

Since there is enough food in the world for everyone, no one has to worry about having enough to eat, right? Wrong! The world has 7 billion people, and nearly 1 billion go hungry every day. In fact, there are more hungry people in the world than the populations of the United States, Canada, and the European Union combined. As the planet's population increases, the number of hungry people will also rise.

A woman sells produce at a market in Guatemala. Much of the world's food is grown by small farmers and sold at markets such as this one.

FOOD IS LIFE

For thousands of years, people all over the world have practiced **agriculture**, the raising of food. Agriculture, or farming, involves working the soil to grow crops such as corn, beans, or melons. Agriculture also includes raising animals for meat or to provide milk. Some farmers plant trees that produce fruit, nuts, coffee beans, or tea leaves.

Food provides **nutrients**, the vitamins and minerals that enable you to survive and stay healthy. Yet many people cannot afford to buy enough food for themselves and their families. Others do not have land on which to grow the food they need.

More than a thousand women and children wait in line for emergency food aid in a village in Niger, western Africa. Several international organizations exist to provide food to people who suffer from hunger caused by drought or other natural disasters.

Children receive food aid in Malawi, southern Africa.

EMPTY FOOD BOWLS

Even people who have the skills to cultivate their own food can be at risk of starvation. Small farmers are often poor, and when their crops fail or sell at low prices, they go hungry.

Sometimes food in a region becomes extremely scarce. This scarcity is called **famine** and can lead to starvation and even death. When crops that are an area's major source of food fail, famine is a very real danger. Crops can fail for a number of reasons, including poor soil and **drought**— a long period without rain. Plant diseases, insects, extreme weather, and war can also destroy crops and create famine.

Some poor people live in **food deserts**, areas where stores that sell nutritious foods are too far away to reach easily. A food desert can be in the middle of a bustling city, or it can be out in the country. Even in times of plenty for everyone else, people living in a food desert are at risk of going hungry or suffering from various illnesses because the only readily available food is not healthful.

WHERE'S DINNER?

Making sure the world's people have enough to eat involves new ways of thinking about food supply. In cities, for example, people have begun growing food in their yards and even on their roofs. In remote rural areas, people are working to increase food yields by making the most of soil and water resources.

In the following pages you will read about how people in India and in a remote area of Mali are working to build **food security**—continued access to sufficient and nutritious food.

Explore the Issue

1. **Identify** What is agriculture? How do the various aspects of agriculture contribute to the world's food supply?

2. **Analyze Cause and Effect** What factors contribute to the fact that 1 billion people do not have enough food?

Hunger in Our

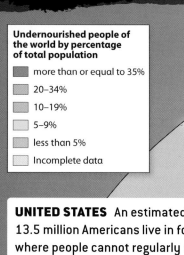

Undernourished people of the world by percentage of total population

- more than or equal to 35%
- 20–34%
- 10–19%
- 5–9%
- less than 5%
- Incomplete data

NORTH AMERICA

NORTH ATLANTIC OCEAN

UNITED STATES An estimated 13.5 million Americans live in food deserts, where people cannot regularly reach sources of nutritious food. Most people living in food deserts have low incomes.

CASE STUDY 2

MALI Many people who live in Mali's rural areas farm to feed themselves. Due to natural disasters, drought, or too little land, they often go hungry.

HAITI Haiti is one of the world's poorest countries. About one-third of Haiti's people suffer from food insecurity, or lack of access to enough nutritious food.

BOLIVIA In Bolivia, one of the poorest countries in Latin America, two-thirds of the people live below the poverty line. Many cannot afford enough food.

SOUTH AMERICA

SOUTH PACIFIC OCEAN

SOUTH ATLANTIC OCEAN

Explore the Issue

1. **Interpret Maps** Which continent has the largest number of countries colored in red? What does this mean?

2. **Make Inferences** What are two important causes of poor nutrition in the world?

World

Study the map below to learn about the nearly 1 billion people throughout the world who are suffering from hunger.

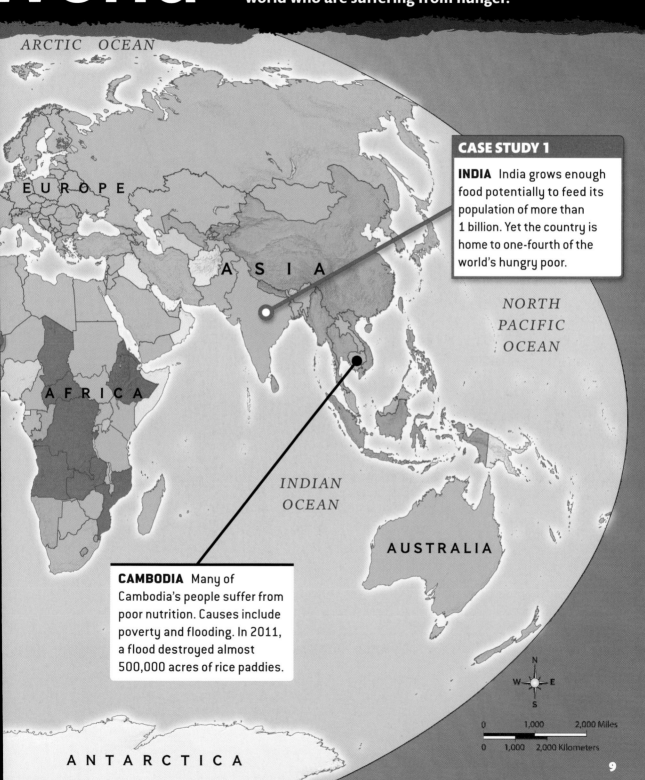

ARCTIC OCEAN

EUROPE

ASIA

AFRICA

NORTH PACIFIC OCEAN

INDIAN OCEAN

AUSTRALIA

ANTARCTICA

CASE STUDY 1

INDIA India grows enough food potentially to feed its population of more than 1 billion. Yet the country is home to one-fourth of the world's hungry poor.

CAMBODIA Many of Cambodia's people suffer from poor nutrition. Causes include poverty and flooding. In 2011, a flood destroyed almost 500,000 acres of rice paddies.

N
W—E
S

| 0 | 1,000 | 2,000 Miles |

| 0 | 1,000 | 2,000 Kilometers |

Feeding INDIA'S People

The majority of tea plantation workers in India are women. Tea plantations such as this one in the state of Kerala often provide housing, water, and other supplies to their workers. Thus, these women may depend on the plantation not just for their pay but to meet other needs as well.

MILLIONS SUFFER FROM HUNGER

India has the world's second largest population: more than 1 billion people. The nation also has a long history of famine that continues to this day. An estimated 20 percent of India's huge population suffers from hunger. That includes the largest number of hungry children in the world.

STRUGGLING WITH HUNGER

Tea grown in the vast, mountainous fields of Assam and Darjeeling is prized throughout the world. India produces more than one-third of the tea grown on the planet. Yet even amidst the lush greenery of the tea fields, poverty and hunger exist. The average pay for a tea laborer is only about one dollar a day.

In recent years, several tea plantations have closed, leaving former workers without even that low wage. These workers and their families are at risk of starvation.

In Uttar Pradesh, another Indian state, hunger is a constant situation for many. Poor children in the village of Ganne, for example, may get one meal a day, or sometimes even less. The children go to a nearby quarry, which is a place where stone is cut out of the ground for uses such as building. There, they eat mud and bits of silica, a mineral. Eating silica causes kidney failure. However, families in Ganne have no money to pay for lifesaving treatments when their children get sick from eating the mineral. Says a worried villager, "We live on a day-to-day basis. What we earn is what we spend on our families in a day."

Many experts believe that India can afford to feed at least a basic diet to all of its people, but distributing food to the people who need it most is a complicated problem. Often food that is intended for the hungry is stolen or misdirected before it can arrive. The Indian government and private organizations are working to solve the problem of providing food for everyone.

GREEN TO THE RESCUE

During the 1960s, reports of widespread hunger in India led people throughout the world to take action. Their concerns led to the **Green Revolution**, a movement aimed at helping India's farmers raise more food.

The Green Revolution focused on Punjab, a state in northern India and the country's main agricultural region. Punjabi farmers began using pesticides and chemical fertilizers. In addition, they used new seeds for wheat, rice, and cotton, which yielded larger crops.

During the 1960s and 1970s, the Green Revolution seemed to be working. Between 1960 and 1980, wheat and rice production increased substantially. But in the 1990s, the growth began to slow. Today experts caution that Punjab is in danger of becoming a "dust bowl," where little if anything will grow.

LIMITS OF THE GREEN REVOLUTION

The Green Revolution eventually created serious problems for Indian agriculture. The Revolution's high-yield crops require more water than rainfall provides. Farmers began digging wells to tap into the **groundwater** that lies beneath Earth's surface. Unfortunately, the water at deeper levels contained salt, which poisoned crops.

This well is in the drought-ridden village of Natwarghad.

Over time, high-yield crops used up the soil's nutrients, substances that plants need to grow. India's farmers started using more chemical fertilizers to replace the nutrients. To pay for more fertilizer and well drilling, farmers had to borrow large amounts of money. As a result, many farmers slipped deeply into debt.

This parched land in the state of Tripura was once a farmer's field. Farming practices that stress the land, combined with natural causes such as drought, have brought about scenes such as this one in various parts of India.

PRODUCTION OF RICE AND WHEAT IN PUNJAB, INDIA, 1961–2006
IN METRIC TONS

	RICE	WHEAT
2005–2006	14,600	10,200
2000–2001	15,600	9,100
1990–1991	12,100	6,600
1980–1981	7,700	3,200
1970–1971	5,100	700
1960–1961	1,800	200

Source: State of Environment Punjab, 2007

A SEARCH FOR SOLUTIONS

Can a second Green Revolution solve India's food problems? Some experts think so. However, they caution that a new revolution must promote **sustainability**—wise use of resources to avoid using them up.

One recommendation is to produce more nutrition-rich crops, such as fruits and vegetables. Another is to raise more poultry or **livestock**—animals raised for their meat or milk—and to establish fisheries. Some experts propose a switch to organic farming, which does not use chemical fertilizers. Others point out that money is needed to support research to improve crop production and build roads so that farmers can transport their produce. Better government policies could ensure a more equal distribution of water and increase opportunities for the rural poor to acquire land and credit.

NO SINGLE ANSWER

Just as there is no single crop that can thrive everywhere, there is no single solution to hunger in India. Projects that address local needs seem to have the best chance of success.

The World Food Programme of the United Nations has begun one such project in the state of Madhya Pradesh. The project's goal is to improve the health of the Sahariya (Sah-huh-REE-yuh) tribe. The women and children of the tribe suffer from **malnutrition**, poor health due to lack of adequate food. Many Sahariya families are so poor their children must work instead of attending school. Eleven-year-old Shiva Adivasi, for example, works 12 hours a day at a roadside tea stall.

The World Food Programme project provides a nutritious powder that people mix with wheat before they grind it into flour. Shiva says that eating food made with the fortified flour has made him feel stronger. Projects such as this one give hope to children throughout India.

Explore the Issue

1. **Analyze Cause and Effect** What were the positive and negative effects of the Green Revolution?

2. **Draw Conclusions** Why is sustainability necessary for a new Green Revolution?

Improved water management techniques helped reclaim this field from desert conditions in the drought-prone state of Rajasthan.

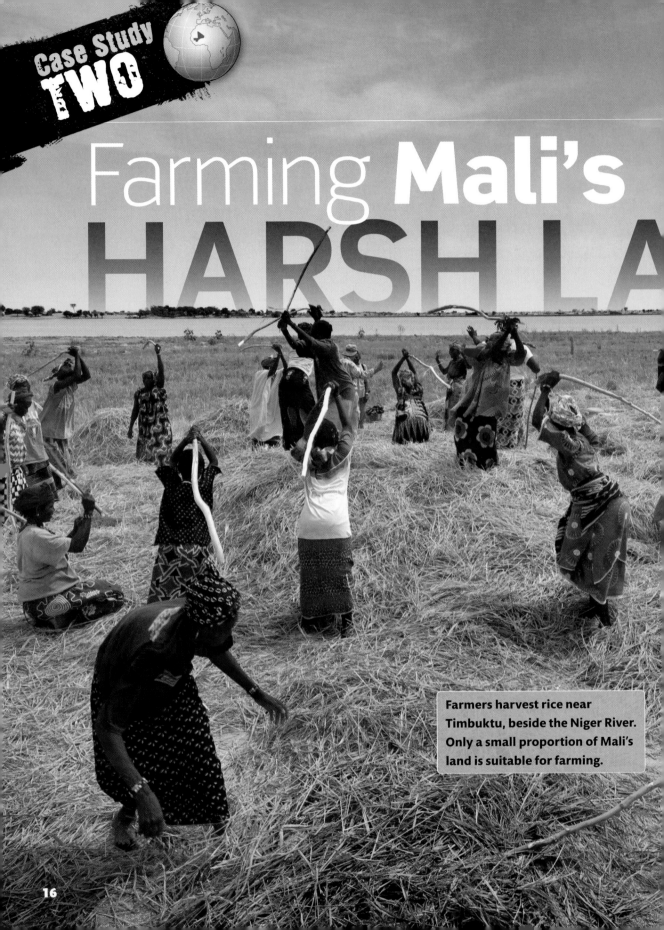

Farming Mali's
HARSH LA

Farmers harvest rice near Timbuktu, beside the Niger River. Only a small proportion of Mali's land is suitable for farming.

RAVE REVIEWS FOR THE DOGON SHALLOT

Even in the food world, onions generally don't create much excitement. But when women from a remote part of Mali—in western Africa—traveled to a food conference in Burkina Faso, food experts took notice. The women's locally grown onions, called **shallots**, took first prize.

The women belong to the Dogon (DOH gahn), an ancient people living in east central Mali on the Dogon Plateau. This part of Mali has suffered environmental stresses and is not hospitable to agriculture. Still, Dogon women have learned to cultivate this useful crop. The quality of their shallots is an example of agricultural success in a harsh land.

The Dogon shallots are not just tasty, they are also a nutritious food. They are low in saturated fat, cholesterol, and sodium—all substances that can cause health problems. At the same time, the shallots contain vitamins A, B6, and C, in addition to manganese, folate, and potassium. The Dogon consume the shallots for their good taste and nutritional value, and they sell them for cash. Growing shallots helps the Dogon feed themselves and also improve their lives by purchasing other goods they need.

FEEDING THE PEOPLE

Located in the interior of western Africa, Mali is nearly twice the size of Texas and is landlocked—surrounded on all sides by land. Most of the country's land area is desert and receives little rainfall. Less than 4 percent of the land is suitable for farming, and crop yields have been falling steadily. Although agriculture accounts for 80 percent of Mali's labor force, it only contributes between 35 and 45 percent of the country's gross domestic product. The term **gross domestic product**, or **GDP**, means the value of all the goods and services produced by a country in a year. Food imports help to feed the country's population of more than 14 million.

Mali is one of the 25 poorest countries in the world. It must depend on aid and loans from other countries to continue functioning. Improvements in agriculture and other industries may hold the key not just to feeding Mali's people but to making the country self-sufficient as well.

POORER SOIL, LESS FOOD

In Mali, as in much of Africa, soil fertility is decreasing, making food harder to grow. Several factors contribute to this condition. One is that farmers can no longer afford chemical fertilizers.

Another is an expanding population. As more people build homes, they take up land that would otherwise be used for crops. As a result, farmers no longer can let land sit idle. Letting farmland sit idle for a period helps it regain its fertility.

The reduction in cattle herds is another factor. People are selling off their cattle in order to turn grazing land into cropland. Fewer cattle mean a shortage of animal manure, which fertilizes crops.

On the Dogon Plateau, soil is thin and often erodes, exposing underlying rock. Cropland is scarce. The climate is hot and dry, and droughts are frequent. Yet the Dogon successfully raise millet, a grain grown for food. They harvest more millet per acre than people in other regions of Africa with similar climate and soil conditions.

A SYSTEM THAT WORKS

The Dogon have learned how to manage their limited soil and water resources wisely. Perhaps the best example is their use of green manure and cover crops to enrich the soil.

Green manure is plant material that replaces nutrients in the soil. The Dogon make green manure by planting trees in their fields. Each year they trim the lower branches before the rains are expected. The branches fall to the ground and fertilize the fields.

Plants that improve soil for farming are called **cover crops**. Dogon farmers plant cover crops alongside food crops. For example, the Dogon plant cowpeas in the same fields as millet. When the cowpeas die, their nutrients enrich the soil for the millet.

In addition, the Dogon employ traditional methods, such as terraces, which are ridges in hillsides that prevent erosion. By building small stone walls to keep the soil in place, they can plant crops on the sides of hills.

In Mali, as in much of Africa, soil fertility is decreasing, making food harder to grow.

Gardens bloom in Segou, Mali. The earthen ridges between the garden plots help retain water.

A man displays a recently harvested shallot.

Dogon women grow millet, a grain, as well as shallots. Here, they pound millet into flour.

GETTING THE MOST FROM SHALLOTS

Dogon shallots grow along small ridges of rocks or soil built to make more water available. Where the land is rocky, farmers use stones to build small, square gardens. They fill the squares with soil and compost and then plant the shallots. Compost is organic material such as leaves and stems that has decomposed and can be used to fertilize the soil.

In spite of all these precautions, poor cultivation and inadequate storage sometimes cause shallots to spoil. Recently, organizations such as USAID and Slow Food International have begun helping the Dogon increase shallot yields and process them more efficiently.

Traditionally, Dogon women have ground shallots by hand. Then they shape the shallot paste into a pellet or ball and leave it in the sun to dry. New mechanical grinders have increased production from 50 kilograms per day to 1 ton per hour.

ENTERING THE GLOBAL MARKET

More efficient processing has enabled Dogon women to sell their products worldwide. At the 2009 food conference in Burkina Faso, Dogon shallots not only took first prize but were in serious demand. One woman received an order for 25 tons!

Dogon traditional flavorings, known as *somè* (SOH-meh), are also drawing attention. The Dogon women create the powdered seasonings from the leaves, flowers, and fruits of shallots and other local plants. Dogon community leader Mamadou Guindo is working to market *somè* at food fairs in Europe.

Selling *somè* outside of Mali will earn money for the Dogon and will help increase their food security. As demand for their products grows, the Dogon will continue to grow the local plants that provide the ingredients. They will be able to feed themselves while sharing their bounty with the world beyond their borders.

Explore the Issue

1. **Find Main Ideas** What is the greatest threat to the food supply in Mali? Explain.

2. **Evaluate** What are the advantages of the green manure and cover crop system employed by the Dogon?

A "Green" Approach to Relieving Hunger

A woman harvests lettuce during the dry season in Dunkassa, Benin. Solar powered drip irrigation has allowed people to grow nutritious vegetables during the long 8-month dry season.

FAR FROM SIMPLE

Environmental scientist Jennifer Burney is concerned that solutions to world hunger may contribute to a different problem—**climate change**, or the gradual warming of Earth's temperatures. In turn, climate change adds complexity to the challenge of defeating hunger.

Growing food can create pollution. Runoff water from irrigation may wash chemical fertilizers and pesticides into lakes and streams. Tractors and other fuel-driven farm equipment produce greenhouse gases that heat up the planet.

As Earth warms, weather patterns become more irregular, making crops harder to grow. More frequent hurricanes and other forms of extreme weather cause intense rains, which cause flooding.

Jennifer Burney works with villagers in Africa.

Progress and growth in agriculture can bring great benefits, creating a more plentiful and varied food supply. Yet the consequences of that progress, as you have just learned, can be harmful. As a National Geographic Emerging Explorer, Jennifer Burney is working with the Society to find a balance. She is striving to reduce hunger while protecting the environment. In sub-Saharan Africa, she works with poor farmers struggling to raise food. "We are a world of plenty, yet almost a billion people don't have enough to eat," notes Burney.

HARNESSING THE SUN

At a test site in Benin (BEH-nin) in West Africa, Burney has tapped into the sun's energy to power irrigation systems. With support from the Solar Electric Light Fund, she has helped set up solar-powered water pumps that regulate the amount of water the irrigation systems receive. On sunny days the pumps work faster, and on cloudy days they work slower. This ensures that the crops, which need more water on sunny days, get the amount of water they need. Since no fuel is burned to produce power, no pollutants are released into the air.

Three years after its installation, the system has improved the farmers' lives. They are able to grow greater quantities of fruits and vegetables. They have more money to buy food and to send their children to school.

CLEANER COOKING

According to Burney, reducing the harmful effects of cooking on the environment is also important. Cooking uses about 8 percent of global energies, and in developing nations, cooking is especially inefficient. Stoves traditionally used in these countries burn wood or dung, which creates soot. When soot is released in homes, it can make people ill. Outside, the black particles can seriously harm the environment. Soot speeds up the melting of glaciers, alters monsoon cycles, and contributes to global warming.

In India, Burney is working on a project to replace traditional cooking stoves with more efficient ones. Early results indicate that the eco-stoves release fewer emissions into the air. They also require less fuel.

Jennifer Burney believes that replacing traditional stoves is the most effective way to immediately begin slowing climate change. It's a simple change that could matter a great deal.

MAKE A DIFFERENCE

As Burney notes, hunger will not be relieved through one grand, sweeping solution. In each part of the world, different factors contribute to hunger, and each solution must be weighed against possible consequences.

You can join in the search for solutions to hunger. First, learn all you can about the issues. Read up on how and where food is raised, nutrition, climate change, and other matters relating to hunger. Decisions made anywhere on Earth about food production and land use affect you, so understand what's happening.

You can also find ways to take action. The activity on the next two pages can help you be part of the solution to hunger in your own community.

Jennifer Burney and farmers in Bessassi, Benin, inspect the farmers' solar-powered water pumps.

Explore the Issue

1. **Analyze Causes** What is the relationship between agriculture and the environment?

2. **Identify Problems and Solutions** Why does Jennifer Burney believe that cooking with eco-stoves in developing nations can slow climate change?

"We are a world of plenty, yet almost a billion people don't have enough to eat." —Jennifer Burney

A woman in West Africa uses a solar cooker to prepare a meal. Unlike some traditional stoves, a solar cooker does not release harmful substances into the air.

Volunteer
at a Community Garden
—and share your results

The solution to world hunger may begin at home. Get involved by volunteering at a community garden and raising fresh fruits and vegetables. The healthy food you grow will help feed hungry people in your part of the world.

IDENTIFY

- Research local community gardens that grow produce.

- Phone or visit the gardens you are interested in to find out about the different tasks you might be asked to do.

- Get the facts. Ask how much food the garden typically produces each year and how it is distributed to those who need it.

ORGANIZE

- Figure out how much time you can devote to the community garden each week and make a schedule.

- Gather whatever tools you'll need for your work in the garden, such as gloves, shovels, rakes, and trowels.

- Recruit friends and family members who are also willing to work in the community garden during the growing season.

A teacher and her students tend the garden they have planted at their school. These herbs and vegetables could help feed people in the community.

DOCUMENT

- Take before, during, and after photos of the community garden and videos of work sessions.

- Keep a record of what is planted in the community garden as well as yields for each type of herb, fruit, or vegetable.

- Jot down your experiences with the plants, the work, and your fellow volunteers and note what you learned in a journal.

SHARE

- Use your photos and videos to create a multimedia presentation of the community garden project and show it to your class.

- Propose that your school start a community garden project that students can help organize and run.

- Write an article for your local paper describing your volunteer work and how it made a difference to you and your community.

Write a How-To Guide

You have volunteered at a community garden in which you helped grow food. Draw on that experience and do some further research to write a how-to guide for others who wish to plant a garden. A clear, well-written gardening guide may inspire friends and family members to start growing food themselves.

RESEARCH

Use the Internet, books, and articles as well as your own experiences in a community garden to research and answer the following questions:

- What soil and sun conditions are best for growing produce in your community?
- When is the best planting time for these food crops?
- How much water and fertilizer do the plants need?

As you do your research, be sure to take notes. Check your sources for accuracy and credibility.

DRAFT

Review your notes and then write a first draft.

- Introduce your topic clearly, previewing what is to follow in your how-to guide.
- Use bullet points to list the steps in the gardening process. Develop the steps using relevant facts and concrete details from your experience in the garden.
- Use appropriate transitions to clarify the relationships among your ideas and the steps in the process.
- Inform your readers using precise language and vocabulary that is specific to gardening.
- In the last paragraph, provide a concluding statement that follows from and supports the information you presented in your introduction and step-by-step list.

REVISE & EDIT

Read your first draft to make sure that it provides step-by-step information on starting a garden.

- Do you clearly introduce the topic of your how-to guide?
- Do the steps contain helpful, relevant, and concrete information?
- Are the transitions between the steps clear and easy to follow?
- Do you use precise, gardening-specific language?
- Does your conclusion sum up and support the information and explanations in your guide?

Revise the how-to guide to make sure you have covered all the bases. Then check your paper for errors in spelling and punctuation.

PUBLISH & PRESENT

Now you are ready to publish and present your how-to guide. Add any images that may help explain the steps you describe. Then print out your guide or write a clean copy by hand. Consider placing the guide in your school library for others to use.

Visual GLOSSARY

agriculture

food security

agriculture *n.*, the growing of food

climate change *n.*, gradual changes in Earth's temperatures

cover crop *n.*, crop planted to enrich the soil

drought *n.*, a long period without rain

famine *n.*, an extreme scarcity of food

food desert *n.*, a place where there is no nearby source of healthful food

food security *n.*, continued access to sufficient and nutritious food

green manure *n.*, plant material that replenishes the soil

Green Revolution *n.*, a movement to help farmers in India raise more food

gross domestic product (GDP) *n.*, the value of all the goods and services produced by a country in a year

groundwater *n.*, water below Earth's surface

livestock *n.*, animals raised for meat or milk

malnutrition *n.*, poor health caused by a lack of adequate food

nutrient *n.*, a substance that living things need to survive and grow

shallot *n.*, a type of onion

sustainability *n.*, wise use of resources to avoid using them up

sustainability

drought

livestock

INDEX

SKILLS

FOOD SUPPLY

THE
GLOBAL ISSUES
SERIES

 CLIMATE CHANGE

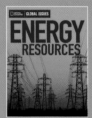 ENERGY RESOURCES

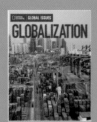 GLOBALIZATION

 HABITAT PRESERVATION

 HEALTH

 HUMAN RIGHTS

 MIGRATION

 POLLUTION

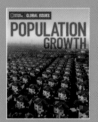 POPULATION GROWTH

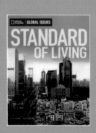 STANDARD OF LIVING

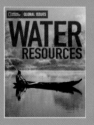 WATER RESOURCES

NATIONAL GEOGRAPHIC LEARNING | CENGAGE Learning

888-915-3276   NGL.Cengage.com

ISBN 978-0-7362-9756-1

90000>

9 780736 297561

ENERGY
RESOURCES

Inspiring people to
care about the planet

– Mission of the National Geographic Society

ABOUT THIS SERIES

The *Global Issues* series supports the National Geographic mission by exploring 21st-century geographic issues that affect countries across the world. Each of the books shown on the back cover of *Energy Resources* focuses on a contemporary challenge in two different regions of the world. Those challenges are common to all of us, no matter where we live. In fact, it's not where a problem occurs that is important—it's how we work together to solve it. Even big problems can be solved through human effort, commitment, and education.

ABOUT THE ISSUE OF ENERGY RESOURCES

Energy use is one of the key issues of our time. People have traditionally relied on fossil fuels, including oil, coal, and natural gas. There are growing concerns, though, about the pollution caused by these energy resources. In addition, these sources of energy are nonrenewable. That is, they can be used up. Countries around the world are exploring ways to use renewable sources of energy, such as solar power. *Energy Resources* examines the role of traditional sources of energy and the development of alternative energy resources.

Multiple power lines transport energy in the form of electricity to Christchurch, one of the most populous cities in New Zealand. (cover)